Imprisoned In Blue

**Written By
Amos Mac, Jr.**

Books may be purchased in quantity and/or special
sales by contacting the publisher, Amos Mac, Jr. by
email at AmosMacJr@yahoo.com.

Published by: Mac Visionz

Interior Design by: iZiggy Promotions

Cover Design by: Dynasty's Cover Me

Editing by: LaShawn Walls, iZiggy Promotions

Formatting by: iZiggy Promotions

ISBN: 978-0-692-31780-8

First Edition

Printed in USA

Acknowledgements

I want to acknowledge all the people who feel imprisoned by the system; everyone who feels they are the targets of the injustices done by the system. To you all, keep pressing forward to your goals. I dedicate this book to the cops out there risking their lives every day doing the right thing and never getting any appreciation, the ones who are still in the field feeling that their work is a no win situation because no one understands, the ones who want out but stay because this work is all they know, and the ones who feel like I do but stay quiet. This is for you all. I appreciate you all!

'A walk down memory lane can unlock the doors or make you a prisoner for life'

MY WORDS

I hope my words cut a deep incision in you and
keloid your thoughts
So that my diction is a constant reminder
Which leaves you hostage
And forces you to face issues that you'd rather be
free from
Hoping it's all an illusion like Dynamo
Only to play on your willingness to be deceived
I hope my words fixate you on the tracks of
emotion
Up and down, through loops and corkscrews
As they blast you until you feel nauseated
I hope my words piss you off, I hope they rile you
up
Make you sad, make you uncomfortable
Make you excited
I hope my words......

VOICE

Let me be vocals of the voiceless,
The ones who work quietly, because they have
few choices.
The ones shouting in silence, within a realm of
racial scrutiny,
Where all parties know the wrongdoings,
But my people have to keep our opinions
between you and me,
The ones who are a threat simply because of
their skin.
Hopefully, my words are an extension of your
cries,
And I realize real lies,
Being quiet while I'm alive is being non-existent
prior to my demise.

Amos Mac, Jr.

SUSPECT'S CRY

Fuck you bruh! Putting me in these bullshit ass cuffs!

Nigga don't try to give me advice, you put me in the back of this car,

Nigga you've done enough!

He trying to act cool using slang, this slave for the white man is phony.

He talking about he feel me, that motherfucka don't even know me,

He don't know my struggle and how no one loves me,

Or about no matter how hard I try, I can't get a job.

What am I left to do but hustle, steal or rob?

That's all I know and him talking hope is a joke,

I already know by age 25 I'm probably going to be in the pen or dead.

What the fuck are my options, I'm not gone starve,

So regardless, I'm getting this bread.

As a youth I knew my destiny, my dad wasn't around

And moms abandoned me for some weak ass clown.

The streets raised me with no guidance,

Now I'm supposed to listen to advice from this
black cop?
Who rolled up on me with the lights and sirens?
Fuck outta here!

Amos Mac, Jr.

TRAITOR

Is this my job description or some other agenda?
Because my gut is saying this ain't right.
Despite 'protecting & serving' these streets at
night,
I'm viewing the arrest files in a different light.
I mean I had suspicion, but never had the
statistics.
The writing has been on the wall, I'm guessing
the generations missed it;
SIX times the incarceration rates of whites,
Black men the odds of us being jailed is likely.
I'm disgusted because everyone I handcuff look
just like me,
And our sentences are roughly TEN percent
longer.
While the households are depleted, black
families are no longer getting stronger,
So where does that leave me?
A tool used in this grand scheme,
Condoning in a sense, because I'm playing on
this team.
The one which equality doesn't apply to all
human beings;
Walking the straight and narrow, yet
I'm a Benedict Arnold it seems.

THUG

It's nothing new under the sun,
But if I ever have a son.
I pray to God his life isn't a tragic one.
No matter the accomplishments or ambitions,
He will be labeled by others like it's their life's
mission.
For instance, this demeaning term has been here
for years.
Recently, been used as a greeting amongst some
peers.
So as we try to disguise it like foundation;
Turning the definition from a negative to a
positive.
Don't think the labelers are using the same logic.
Such a horrendous word which is now used as
endearment;
Is masked in plain sight like clansmen who don't
revere it.
It's only used to describe a certain demographic;
Insulting our intelligence as if we don't know
what's happening.
I witness it from coworkers, only black criminals
are called this,
Even though we represent the same badge.
I know how you really feel regardless,
Some things will never change.

They are embedded like blood stains on a rug,
NIGGER is now better known as thug.

LOW PRIORITY

Can anyone explain?
Why tragedy has to occur like someone being slain?
In the black community before suspects are held accountable,
A lot of subjects are walking around,
With their arrest history being insurmountable,
Like this one fella with ten felonies.
Most are gun charges, B&Es and robberies;
His last case was an armed jacking.
Two months later he murdered a black guy.
It seems like the law is slacking.
What I'm asking;
Is if his prior crimes were against a wealthy white person,
Would this homicide have had a chance to happen?

CALL 911

It's nothing new; I know how you feel 'fuck 12!'
We hear it all the time,
I just hope you can count to a higher number, I
thought to myself.
As we approached this frequent flyer dressed in
all black,
A typical interaction with the 5-0 hating, I get
money and bitches,
This is my block character;
As usual we were of no use to him,
Like peasants entering his throne having the
audacity to part our lips,
To speak in his presence, hearing the shouts of
'we don't need y'all, get the fuck out!'
As we left the neighborhood, feeling like players
from an opposing team in a hostile venue,
The night continues with all types of calls for
service.
Nearing 1a.m. the dispatch sends us back to the
previously mentioned neighborhood,
'I bet that's 'ol boy again' we said in a bored
manner;
Due to experiencing this same episode over and
over like Matlock reruns.
While approaching the apartment, this grim
feeling of evil entrenched my body,

The door was open to the apartment, but there
was a chill in the air that cooled this humid
night,
We stepped through the door's threshold not
knowing what to expect;
Weed baggies, crack rocks and cash were
scattered all over the floor
As I looked behind the sofa I saw a lifeless body
dressed in all black,
The carpet was soaked with blood as brain
fragments sprinkled the floor,
The call was for 'ol boy, but this time death
reached him first.
In the form of a projectile ignited by gun powder
to his head,
We discovered his girlfriend and daughter
upstairs, petrified with fear.
Horrified, the girlfriend trembled as she relived
his last moments;
She uttered, "I looked out of the window and saw
a guy come in the house
I didn't pay much attention, but moments later
he yelled the last words
That I would ever hear come out of his mouth,"
as she cried.
What did he say ma'am?
She replied,
'BABY, CALL THE POLICE!!'

VIEWER'S CHOICE

They say believe nothing what you hear and only
half of what you see,
So anytime a police video comes out, people start
questioning me.
You feel because I'm a cop I always agree.
It's not the case, but understand you should
always check the source;
Persuasion of viewers is always the uploader's
choice.
I've yet to see much media who is pro-police,
Even with our good far exceeding the bad.
That positive imagery, you'll never see;
The local news rather display police controversy,
Instead of showing a slain officer's anniversary,
I think it's just me, but I thought public service
was a team affair,
It took this experience for me to become aware,
That in this game there has to be a villain
And I guess since I took this job,
I was one who was willing,
To be a 'bad' good guy, trying to win over
civilians.
Like a theatrical script, but the film is still
rolling,
And I'm fighting a losing battle,
By patrolling.

THE PRICE

It's like an oxymoron; I mean I'm not a criminal,
But this treatment says otherwise.
 I understand a subliminal I took an oath for this
badge,
But what does that mean?
It doesn't mean us and the courts are on the
same team.
I get paid to risk my life and trusted with a pistol.
Yet, in courtrooms my honor code isn't looked at
as official.
My word means nothing; I'm wrong for doing my
job,
I feel I'm a defendant and my trial is being
robbed.
I'm only a number here that's plain to see,
I risk my life daily yet, it takes ten years for the
department to invest in me.
How can it be you value my worth?
When I'm monitored by GPS each day I'm at
work.
It's no love here you place all liability on me,
So when I'm troubled enforcing your orders,
I'm sued or jailed while your hands are washed
free.
So, with that in mind I pray to make it home
safe,

Amos Mac, Jr.

I came here for honor,
Learned quickly this isn't the place.

ONLY ME

A geyser brewing and ready to explode at
Yellowstone,
Is a valid comparison to the internal friction,
Housed within this 6-foot frame of dark flesh,
Which on a daily contemplates why bother
Strapping that body armor over his chest
And working amidst his community even though
they detest.
His whole existence, not realizing he's one of the
few who will listen.
Originally believing police work was his mission
Of assisting a decaying element;
Which was strategically placed in position
To destroy the black community, unbeknownst
to him.
He's wrong and simply the enemy,
Extremism on both sides often collide, so there's
the bottle
To the side at times in which he confides.
His peers don't understand and most coworkers
stick to the plan,
He feels he's simply a grain in the sand,
Because he's only one man.
He's in this position because
He won't be reprogrammed.

MISUSED

How can I hide behind the badge?
When I'm just a 'nigger' in uniform.
A slave to my bills, a slave to a job which I feel
Instills a falsehood of brotherhood, I'm
imprisoned with this job.
Ironically, I assist with the imprisonment of
others,
I feel like I'm working against my brothas,
Like I'm some sort of slave arresting coons while
saying yes masash.
Am I being overly dramatic and is this
farfetched?
Not nearly, just correlate the black population.
In regards to the arrests yearly,
It's been forever skewed, us being screwed
And I'm helping that cause working here,
Talents being misused.

THE PRESCRIPTION

Many of my coworkers confide in you
Because you seem to always be there
To listen when no one else does.
They get a kick out of you, their life's buzz.
You work in silence, but I question your
counseling
Because your patients at time become violent.
After your sessions, some cry and become
talkative,
But there's few progression.
In the aftermath of their problems, they seek you
out for comfort,
But your diagnosis makes things worse
Because your mirage of an escape is a curse;
Which leads to drowning in your toxic liquid.
Everyone knows the outcome that follows when
becoming intimate
With the bottle.

CALL FOR SERVICE

I walk towards you only with good intentions
And I understand your circumstances, did I forget the mention?
I'm no different; I'm just working towards a pension.
My livelihood is the reason we're meeting here this instance.
We're strangers, yet I'm prejudged;
Before this current title people showed me love.
Now its insults, fuck you and jokes;
Ironic, I became this to assists the folks.
So we're face to face and to you I'm a disgrace
A sellout, an Oreo, you should spit in my face.
That's your thoughts right, well I'm only assuming,
Our relationship with the public has already been ruined.
Way before I came, to most I'm one and the same,
But this is public service, so I continue playing this game.
Calling 911, with urgency is the manner in which I came,
You don't believe it, as usual I'm the one to blame.
As I continue walking I see the look in your eyes,

They're full of anger and displeasure, another angry customer.
All I can say is 'Sir, how may I help ya?'

BLAME GAME

Stop blaming the blue line and take some
responsibility.
I didn't make you make your decisions,
So, miss me with the hostility.
Check this possibility, is it possible you robbed
some kid,
Punched your baby mom's in the face; in front of
your kids?
Fool, you deserve that bid, but you blame me,
Like I put a battery in your back, you're not
hypnotized,
You're misguided in fact,
In this world there's cause and effect.
You got caught with coke, so you know confined
time comes with that.
So; your blame turns to anger, towards me; a
stranger,
Who vowed to help the public when it comes to
danger?
It's cool we all play our positions,
But understand your actions are why you're in
this patrol car,
Shackled in that handcuffed position.

10-88

What exactly is an 88? Better known as a
suspicious person.
I mean, why are they suspicious?
Are they termed that because of their living
conditions?
For instance, the brass ordered us to get out with
everyone one night.
So, basically everyone was suspicious that night.
I realize this is a high crime location,
But this community isn't all criminal;
We'd be searching out of desperation,
Stopping people at the Shell gas station and the
Lotto players hoping to win a few bucks.
It's funny because no cops are stopping people
On the rich side of town, showing up at
Starbucks,
True, they don't have half of the crime
It's because those residents have way more than
a dime.
To their name, I grew up with little money and
even right now, it's still the same.
I wasn't suspicious back then, neither am I now,
But it's no wonder why residents don't trust us
when we come around.
A low income area with no jobs, amongst
violence,

A bad hand was dealt, yet they're all treated like criminals and expected to be silent.

KILLER

Anytime an officer kills someone,
I'm always questioned about my thoughts or
opinion,
Like I was a part of it and knew the situation.
They await my response with some sort of
fascination,
But the questions only arise when a white cop
kills an unarmed black person.
The cop is not prosecuted.
I simply respond,
If I killed an unarmed white person, it's a no
brainer,
I wouldn't be surprised if I was executed.

COP'S LOVE

Come on baby, you know we can't be seen
together right now;
Especially, while I'm in uniform.
You know I'll catch all type of heat if people see
us with each other,
I'd just be reinforcing the stereotype.
I know you are attracted to men in uniform,
more so cops,
But our relationship has to be on the Hush!
Hush!
So, let's keep our encounters on lock,
I must admit though, I love your sexy frame.
With a round bottom resembling a perfect circle
or even perhaps an 'O'.
Lotion that makes your skin glisten, better
known as glaze.
We intentionally don't make eye contact when
I'm wearing the badge,
So, it's unsettling when we part ways.
I envision the bliss I feel when we don't have to
hide and share that moment
Such intimacy makes me lust for you.
Let me nibble on you gently when you're feeling
lonely.

You don't understand my reasoning for our bond
being kept in the dark,
Please don't get mad it's not you, it's all on me,
Because what we have the world doesn't need to
see.
Secret lovers, oh how I fiend,
My ode to the lovely Krispy Kreme!

Amos Mac, Jr.

NEIGHBORHOOD DEALER

Is it wrong to view this drug dealer in a different
light;
Despite causing many people not to sleep at
night.
Inflicting such destruction in the hood,
This ruthless menace somehow manages to
instill some good.
He doesn't see the carnage caused by the crack
he sells,
To him by age 26, he thought he would've been
dead or in jail.
So thinking about the future and the
repercussions,
Is not a matter of discussion?
To him, this is the hand he was dealt.
He is consumed by negative energy,
But showing love to younger kids was often his
tendency.
Handing out food in the projects was good logic,
Since his hunger pains weren't far in the past.
For cats that had talent his message was to stay
in class,
Get that education kid, you gone be better than I
am.
Ironically, advice from this hustle reinforced kids
to stick to the program,

Running the streets seemed exciting, especially
from the view of a kid,
But this criminal did some good
He influenced a few lives with a pass and
positivity
Before being shipped off to do his bid.

GROWN MAN

I see you grilling me with that look in your eye,
Like you'd throw the hands if I say something to
you.
What you don't realize is I'm human and a grown
man at that,
So that negative energy you dishing can be
reflected right back.
Yea this is considered a professional position,
But that disrespecting shit for no reason; ain't a
sound decision.
I envision, us speaking as adults.
I'm sorry you had a bad experience with another
cop, but that wasn't my fault.
It wasn't me, it's plain to see and I'm actually
hearing your point.
Thinking to myself, what would I do if that were
me?
See, we have more in common than you think,
But I'm not one to be belittled, let's be frank.
I don't fit the description of that 'Oreo' term you
dishing,
So understand us both being safe is my goal and
plan,
But I'll do what it takes for me to make it home.
Like I said, I'm a grown ass man!

BLACK MEN

Black men, why are our aspirations extinct?
How did we transform into this atrocity in which
we think?
Fellas, we're powerful so we owe it to ourselves
to do better,
It's like the manner of our movement is no
longer clever
Doing the 'IN' thing like sheep walking into
slaughter,
Without a mind of our own, being killed in the
majority by our own.
My skin seems to be my enemy wishing the
downfall upon itself,
Rather support another race than an up and
coming brother needing your help.
Desensitize each other when calling us niggas,
I bet no one ever said 'fuck that brother' before
pulling the trigger.
What happened to the sense of pride in
ourselves?
Now we have more pride in what shoes we buy
off the shelves.
We're a dying species, killing off one another.
Do you really believe that's not a plan?
We participating in the extermination of us,
using our own hands.

Fatherless boys are growing into the same man,
That made them fatherless, abandoning their
seeds with pure cowardice,
I acknowledge this because this is what I see.
We have to do better
We all should be saying, "Change starts with
me!"

CIVILIAN CLOTHES

With great power comes great responsibility,
A quote from a superhero movie I think.
When you carry yourself like ironman
With a vest on your chest and a metal badge
known as a shield,
You feel is some sort of force field,
Responsibility is required, that uniform makes
you feel tough,
Allowing you into places most describe as rough.
A setting in which you don't reside,
Where the citizens survive amidst many not
having 9-5's
And coping with an unwritten code of anything
goes.
I bet you wouldn't visit there in civilian clothes
And bark orders while calling them turds.
It's easy to flex when you're rolling in herds,
With the blue polyester crew, I knew a lot of you
Prior to getting that badge, so stop playing that
roll,
Selling your soul being something you're not,
But since being in the 'hood' is your occupation.
Understand this destination isn't understood by
you or your administration,
So you should expect the people's reaction

When you have the 'hood' interactions.

CURRENT STATE

Dead bodies piling by the day,
Black brothers losing life at an early age,
It's sad this is normal to us like turning a page,
Of a magazine that displays repetitive articles,
But these magazines house hollow points as their arsenal.
Books aren't vests don't protect your chest
And their idea of chess is running the block and pushing a 'Lex,
These are our youth forsaken by adults, barely surviving,
Clinging to life by a thin rope, work to them is selling weed, pills or coke
And the hope that us pigs won't catch 'em in possession of dope.
The question is why does many feel this is the only option,
Like the neighborhood is the only thing popping.
I'm blessed I wasn't subdued by this hood doctrine,
But it's painful seeing the acceptance of the lack of knowledge.
I'm not talking college, more so the seeds being misguided
And the hard lifestyle only being provided.

SAME QUESTION

I hear the same questions constantly,
Like the ringing sound in your ear when
suppressed in complete silence.
Why would you even consider being a cop?
What made you want to do that, what's your
story on becoming a cop?
Outside of stable employment, the answer is
simple,
I set out to be something I never witnessed;
A cop who is familiar with the injustices of
people
And realize it's an agenda and wants to change
the police culture from the inside.
Influence more brothers and sister to 'go blue',
Understanding that black cops could really help
And make a change in our community.
So many people sit back and complain while
placing blame,
I figured I'd become one and treat everyone fair,
With these hopeful thoughts I began this
journey.
Those thoughts have since withered away
In this hallucinatory universe.

FALSE NUMBERS

Numbers are a complex topic,
Which usually describes a particular sum or amount.
What's ironic is sometimes the sum isn't always the proper amount.
For instance, what impresses the command staff in this field is statistics;
The more arrests, field interviews, citations for traffic,
You're considered a hard worker who is proactive.
So oftentimes 'community policing' is downplayed, which is tragic,
There's no 'at a boy' when developing relationships within the neighborhoods.
It's more like, great job using those people to get a confession.
You've done well, I'm not saying arresting criminals isn't a grand relief,
Instead, high arrest numbers doesn't automatically make you a good officer.
What good is it to have impressive stats,
If you're numb to community relations?
In that case, you really are another enemy,
In which the community is facing.

MY JOB

What you don't understand is,
I don't agree with a lot of the things that come
along with my job,
Well, it's more like the vast majority,
And if I don't comply they would no longer
employ me.
You may be saying well,
Why won't you just quit your job?
If that's the case;
I'm asking you the same question.
If it were that easy,
Everyone would have jobs they absolutely loved.
As the world turns, it's about getting that grub,
And feeding your family,
And let's not discuss the economy.
In all actuality, the police were the only ones to
hire me.
Equipped with two degrees and no record.
I did everything I was taught to do,
Yet, I'm in a profession,
Where I'm only liked by a few,
But hated by most,
Why doesn't he just drop his broom?
When the boss is chewing out that worker in that
meeting,
Why doesn't he just storm out the room?

The reality is, we need that paycheck to survive.
We adhere to orders even if we consider them
odd,
So when I arrive on scene don't kill me,
THE MESSENGER,
I'm just doing my job.

DATING A COP

Okay, you say I've changed in regards to you and
our conversations,
Like our growth stopped and 'us' is no longer a
destination.
I admit my schedule has put a strain on our
progression
And my laid back demeanor comes with a little
more aggression.
I used to like talking and coming up with
solutions to your problems,
But that's now my job ten hours a day, listening
to other's problems.
I'm all about relaxation when you come around,
So, of course, when you start complaining
About petty stuff when you see me, I start to
frown.
When you're upset because your coworker keeps
tapping their pen on the desk,
I'd switch places because I rather deal with that
than
Seeing this sixteen year old with a hole in his
chest
And trying to console his cousin who saw his
relative breathe his last breath.

So let's not talk about work, neither one can
relate
And understand my daily experiences has an
effect
On my outlook as of late
I still love you, however this isn't my sole
purpose.
Now, you see why it's hard to date a guy in public
service.

FIRE

Talking to my mom on the phone as I pulled into the gas station.
We were having our typical mom-son talk and she said,
"Baby, how was work last night, did you do anything exciting?"
The odor of gas forced me to relive last night's episode when she asked that.
So I flashed back; my partner and I arrived on scene to an 'assist fire' call.
Simply to secure the perimeter as the firefighters put out a house fire.
Such a cold night full of darkness, the only light visible came from the fire trucks.
There was smoke still coming from the torched vehicle in the driveway.
The house was entrenched in a thick wood line where I could only see the outline of trees
Hovering over the house, a few of us went inside the building,
Bullets were lying all over the floor drenched in gas, which couldn't be absorbed by the carpet.
I felt like I was on a movie set playing a cop role in a cinematic thriller.

There was no one inside the residence; the firefighters had already cleared the house.
We were about to exit the home while some officers made a few jokes,
Before one cop walked towards the sofa in the living room.
There was a big pile of clothes covered by a white sheet on the sofa.
One officer pulled the sheet off of the clothes, but it wasn't actually clothes,
It was a dead body, the body was sitting upright on the knees
With the hands and feet bound together with duct tape.
It appeared as if she had just been murdered, "Oh Shit!" we said.
Paranoia covered me as we left out the house, "The suspect could be anywhere in those woods, ready to pop us without warning" said one cop.
A neighbor tipped us off to where the owner of the house hangs out at times; it was an abandoned house.
Located a few houses down, a squad of us went to the house as tactful as we could at that point.
We found the subject hiding behind a tree, clenching a pistol in his right hand.

While popping pills in his mouth with his left, he
yelled, "I'm not going to jail, you better kill me!"
With our guns drawn, we gave him commands to
drop his weapon.
He continued to say, "Kill me!" This standoff
continued for what seemed like a minute,
But it was as if time had stopped, he then
pointed the gun in our direction.
"Put it down!" a few cops shouted once more, I
saw the crazed look he had in his eyes
As we made eye contact in slow motion, he then
turned the gun on himself and killed himself.
Those eyes were etched in my brain, as his
lifeless body dropped to the ground.
I snapped back to the present as I could hear my
mom echoing in a distance
And her voice became louder saying, "Are you
still there son, how was work, can you hear me?"
I simply replied, "It was cool mom, kinda boring,
nothing really happened last night."

WRONGED

I've always wondered,
How can us cops be right, if we tell suspects
they're doing wrong?
Yet, give them no avenue to do right?
Is it not wrong to scold a person on selling drugs,
Then arrest them, thus giving them a record?
In turn, they have no way of getting a job,
I understand some people deserve to be arrested,
But how can we point a finger
At someone's wrongdoings without providing
Some direction for them to make a change?

US

I don't hate us, I hate the way we've become,
The things we value, have no value.
We used to be thoroughbreds, now we're just
sick in the head.
Just sleep in the bed, is what a lot of us do.
Collecting government checks like it's winning
the lotto.
The current motto, take advantage of the system.
Ignorant to the fact they're dumbing us down,
Making us dependent, so when they end it
We're left in limbo with no way to defend it.
Fend off the hunger, no healthcare, no income,
It'll be like the plague and then some.
Meanwhile, killing each other, 94% of homicides
Are by the hands of another brother.
Why is keeping it real associated with
committing crime?
I'm real because I push weight and supply lines,
So our ancestors fought for freedom and this
dream?
We've got the be the most intelligent, ignorant
people
On the scene.

COP'S TOOL

We first united sometime around the 1850's
And been an item ever since.
We give each other a sort of power
That makes most people sick.
See, a lot of outsiders don't trust our bond.
Our public display of affection is never
questioned,
Due to our cameos on site being expected.
When we hit the scene we get all the attention,
Usually it's in the midst of friction.
I'm really the quiet type
Whereas, my partner is a loud mouth when
things get hype.
Silently, I command respect,
With me, I make people poke out their chest
And some may even flex,
But my other half is a loose cannon.
When provoked, his aggression can lead to
destruction
So, most people follow the instructions, when
he's revealed.
Our presence makes some glad, but more mad.
You see he's the cop's pistol
And I'm the cop's badge.

Amos Mac, Jr.

DISCRETION

In this line of work there is much discretion.
With that in mind I have a question,
Is taking someone to jail over one joint
And him losing his job
Really worth teaching a lesson?

OUTSIDE OF THE UNIFORM

They told me in the academy people only see the
uniform and not you.
When I wear my regular clothes,
I'm unnoticed, so that's true,
But the sad thing is, it applies to some officers
too.
I'm greeted and respected when wearing the
badge,
But when it comes off, I'm treated no different
than I was in the past.
Not surprising, it's been those same cops,
Giving me the shakedown on traffic stops and
Bending the rules before I tell them to stop.
I know you're not following protocol, because I
too am a cop.
Then comes the disbelief staring at me.
"You're a cop?" That's the follow up response,
Yep, we had training together, I met you last
month.
Smiling with a little dismay, he says, "Ohhh! I do
remember
You from the other day, you look like a rap
person
With your bling necklace on display. You have
earrings too,

You should have mentioned it earlier that we met
the other day."
The traffic stop is quickly over and I'm 'allowed'
to go on my way,
But what do you think would've happened
If we never met the other day?

QUEENS

Strong black queens, please unite, because we
need you desperately.
I believe you are the strongest creatures on
Earth,
Why don't you realize your self-worth?
I'm so grateful of the queen in which I was
birthed.
To love, discipline, teach and support me,
That's the survival kit I needed to have a fighting
chance in this cruel world.
You beautiful gems are becoming Ocean Dream
Diamonds,
Stunning, but rare.
 I ache when I see you getting beat by men
And you continue to stay because you feel your
options are few.
You neglect your kids for your current boyfriend
of the month
And exploit your body because entertainment
tells you
This is how y'all are supposed to be, this is how
we come into contact with each other,
Whether by domestic violence incidents,
prostitution on the strip and Backpage,
Along with 'step dad' having sexual encounters
with your daughters,

Because you rather side with a deadbeat than
fight for your seed.
Due to you 'needing' a man, let's do better
queens.
The say the future starts with the kids, I disagree,
It starts with adults, the ones who raises them
up.

RECRUITING GAMES

It's like being a local celebrity, yeah right,
That's what you told me though.
Selling the job like a coach desperate for an
extension.
Playing your strong hand and calling my bluff.
You saw the anticipation in my eyes,
Knowing I had no other option and you preyed
on it.
Concealing the truth, a chameleon of the shield,
You knew what I would experience, yet hid it
from me.
I don't blame you though, because in your eyes,
you were looking out for me,
While presently, I look at you with scorn.
I simultaneously appreciate you for giving me
this opportunity,
Maybe I'm built different as I ponder,
Because I would have chanced a person declining
the position.
Doing my best Van Gogh impersonation,
painting a masterpiece colored by truth.
I wouldn't smile the entire time and mask the
cons only promoting the perks,
Then jerk the rod and have you hooked giving
the term fishermen of men

A whole new meaning, so when you're exposed
to the real,
I reveal I'm not happy and would leave if I could,
damn crabs in a bucket.
You could escape if you wanted and be a
profound salesman,
Because that con job would impress the likes of
James Hogue.
Thank you fellow officers!

HIP HOP

Riding in the coupe, rocking to J. Cole's "Let Nas Down,"
I gaze out the window, sort of like staring out the window pane,
With my 'window pain' in deep thought while switching lanes.
I ponder if hip hop would accept me any longer,
Such a rich culture I grew up listening to Wu,
Nas, Mobb Deep, Mic Geranimo too, that's just a few.
A long list of MCs who had influences on me.
As most know, hip hop isn't fond of pigs,
Look at NWA's 'Fuck Tha Police' what's ironic,
I don't feel like they're talking about me.
Yea, this is my job, but outside of this uniform,
This hip hop lifestyle is my norm.
Run DMC got me hooked on shell toe Adidas, my favorite brand,
While watching Rock Steady Crew on Beat Street doing head stands.
I love hip hop, but I doubt it loves me.
Guess earning this salary, turned me into the enemy.

Amos Mac, Jr.

BOY IN BLUE

He's good people was always the response,
When asked about yours truly,
You could vouch for that if you knew me.
It all changes, when you discover my job,
The slick jokes and your demeanor, now is quite
odd.
Being me is never going to stop; I've known your
lifestyle.
Suddenly you think I'm going to call the cops,
That's comical, this is my job not my life.
When my uniform is off, you think I'm
concerned with your actions,
While I'm trying to sleep at night? And stop
asking me to tell cop stories.
That shit annoys me, my identity is what you see,
and not who employs me.
In fact, I'm at the point where all of this cop shit
bores me,
Most cops only talk police work like it's a 'COPS'
episode,
Even conversations outside of work, they're
using 10-codes.
Chill with that 'hey officer' stuff in public,
Everyone don't need to know what I do.
I'm still the same me with my same name,
Before joining the boys in blue.

COPS AND ROBBERS

What do cops and robbers have in common
Besides, being the subjects of that famous
childhood game?
Me and most robbers have one thing in common,
We both wear masks.
They wear masks to conceal their identity,
In hopes of preventing solitary confinement.
I wear my mask to work to conceal how I really
feel
And remain professional,
While being expected to ignore the obvious.

Amos Mac, Jr.

OFFICER IN THE SCHOOL

Math was never my best subject in school,
But I do know how to add and solve novice
equations.
Working in the school system as an law
enforcement officer
I witnessed a lot of expressions, variables,
propositions, etcetera,
In the form of a school setting,
But this arithmetic doesn't have the proper
annexation.
Why would you start a k-8 public school and
house the students in an elementary school
building?
Thus, creating an overcrowded atmosphere
amongst peers;
Who come from the exact same environment?
A low income area with little to no resources.
Kindergarteners are in school with 7th and 8th
graders,
With ankle monitors who wear it with pride like
a fashion accessory.
Teachers quitting daily because they have no
support from school administration and parents,
So the classroom is a zoo, where hardly any
instruction is taking place.

Creating yet another unstable foundation in the
lives of these children.
They aren't exposed to anything besides their
environment,
It's almost like keeping them closed minded.
Is it really ironic these schools aren't
implemented
On the higher income side of the city?

ARMCHAIR ACTIVISM

Surrounded by the echoes of people,
Saying what they would have done
As if they were in that situation,
How do you know?
Have you ever felt your life was in danger?
And survival depended on swift action in the
blink of an eye?
Radio and television stations, the news and the
general public
Are quick to criticize controversial events,
But what makes you all the experts in the field,
You wouldn't dare partake?
Armchair activism is plaguing the world,
It's easy to sit in the safety of your home and lash
out
The would haves, could haves and should haves
During the aftermath.

EYES OPEN

The environment was odd and somewhat cloudy.
My movement was sluggish and my voice more
rugged.
I was me, but I didn't feel like me.
Everything was strange, I saw myself walking
And that hooded guy jumped out of the Range.
How could I be walking at the same time
watching myself walk?
I thought, not recognizing my own voice when I
talked.
While wearing the uniform I was ambushed,
Bullets tore into my body by surprise,
But I didn't feel pain as I watched my death and
sure demise.
Suddenly, I opened my eyes and realized,
After taking a deep breath, it was a dream.
One of many, after seeing footage of fellow
officers being murdered on screen.
Useful training.

COP-TYPE

I refuse to reinforce the stereotypes,
Like cops ain't cool and they became cops
Because they were picked on in school
Or to be the worst person on the road alive.
Apparently in the movies,
None of us can drive.
It's believed we are all in the police
administration,
Due to our lack of education.
Please, I have degrees and I don't believe I'm
above the law,
But if that's not enough, you can witness I'm not
corrupt.
I admit, as a youth and now as a grown up,
I'm very fond of doughnuts.
Who isn't, that's the norm, but I refuse to
consume while in uniform.
Not a fan of coffee and what is a cop haircut?
I don't have much power to abuse.
Plus, I'm sent to internal affairs if my temper
even flares.
I don't do dip or wear a thick ass mustache above
my lip,
Nor do I turn on my blue lights in order not to
wait at a red light.

I don't pull over cars out of envy, because I can't
afford it
And I'm not J Reid; undercover work isn't like
the movies, I explored it.
Those are a few stereotypes that I don't live up to
And the many more left,
I didn't address.

THE GAME

The drug game is simply that,
A game.
Never ending in pain and sacrifice,
Of people's lives for monetary gain.
Why risk my life chasing after drugs,
I'm not Robocop.
No matter how much drugs I get,
The shit won't stop.
The reasoning,
The streets and the law both benefit....

URBAN SCHOOL

Became a cop to make a difference,
But no difference is made on the beat,
So, I left to work in schools,
Thus, leaving the streets.
All black school, with an all-black
administration,
Saying they'd make much change,
Was the proclamation.
Sadly, the principal walks around with his nose
up,
As if low income residents are beneath him.
Yet, expects them not to explode when he
mistreats them.
Told me he wants kids to fear the badge,
Reinforcing the wrong cop image which is real
sad.
I went there to build relationships with the
troubled youth,
I knew what I was facing.
These aren't 'his people,'
He's accustomed to a white middle to upper class
population,
Zero tolerance for insubordination
With a no bullying zone.
A hypocrite, his actions are that of a bully,
What's really going on?

CONVERSATION

This black officer once said he hates these niggas
out here,
I stared at him with befuddlement and was
perplexed.
I thought, "What the hell is he talking about?"
Then I recalled that fucked up scene in 'Boyz N
Tha Hood'
Where the black cop put a revolver to Trey's
neck.
I grew up thinking that cop was a black dude
racist against his own race.
There are some cops out here like that for sure,
Who don't understand such demographics?
This one in particular, doesn't fit that
description,
His pops was locked up for hustling.
Thus, was never in his life and his mom battled
with her own issues.
He was from the block, so I asked him to clarify
his statement.
He said, "my nigga, I love my black people, but
this black on black
Crime, cats terrorizing people in the same
situation as they are in,

That slave mentality, niggas getting in our faces
when you actually trying to help
Gets old, know what I'm saying?" "How you
flipping on me when
YOU called 911, then be like fuck y'all and argue
with me?
I could've gone the rest of my life and been
happy not seeing and dealing with you.
That's why I say I hate these niggas out here!"

TONIGHT

I knew this wasn't right,
From my first night, my field training officer
Said, "What you need to understand is, our job is
to solve the problem for the night."
It all came to light; no problem is solved in one
night.
The mentality of most here, isn't to solve an
issue,
It's to bandage it lightly, like a wound dressing
made of tissue.

TEMPTATION

Look at all this drug money,
I should take some, nobody would notice.
This is evidence now, that fool is dead he can't
use it,
But a cop stealing drug money is far beyond
foolish,
But what's going to be done with it?
Maybe it'll be locked in property,
Burned or the department spends it.
I'd have to be careful doing dirt because of
forensics.
If I take some, it would be of good use.
I'm underpaid and I risk my life,
Behind on medical bills, because that sickness is
weakening my wife.
My kids deserve better;
Getting picked on in school,
Because I can't afford them new shoes.
It's like our lives are being robbed.
Maybe running into this money is a blessing
from God,
I'm trusted to be honorable, but this life ain't
fair.
At this point my thoughts turn crooked,
But I don't even care.

Amos Mac, Jr.

What's a man to do when his back is against the wall?
Will he do whatever to stand tall?
Or make sure that man doesn't fall?

MAN IN UNIFORM

I know it's really not me it's the rush,
The thrill of a man in uniform on the hush.
You know it can't be an "US,"
Because we both have families.
You have a husband and I have a wife.
My schedule is a great excuse for us to link up at night,
But, your reasoning was you needed a friend.
But we both knew what the outcome would be in the end.
We know this should only be a phase,
But our encounters have been more sentimental the last few days.
This is beyond wrong, this so called secret bond.
I'm a disgrace, I can't even look my child in her face.
What's sad is we never stopped, until we both got caught.
Now we're on the rumor mill a lot,
I'm described as a home wrecker, since I know your husband
He too, is a cop.

Amos Mac, Jr.

TITLE STORY

I believe in God,
So 'it was written' for me to be in this position.
I feel, even though we control our own decisions.
Did I dream of being a cop?
Never, as a kid I watched Kung-Fu flicks.
I could watch 'Wu-Tang forever', I love sports
and watch those more.
No cell phones back then, you had to watch
ESPN to catch 'the score'
Of your favorite team, wasn't exposed too much
but had 'street dreams'.
I was going to be something; I thought, 'Lord
willin' I would be an inspiration to the children.
Unlike O-Dog, I wasn't 'Amerikaz Nightmare',
my parents scolded me,
Saying I had a brain so use it.
My freshmen year of high school, I rode out to
'Murda Muzik.'
My focus was school and ball, getting those
assists, transferred schools.
Didn't know my junior year I would get 'the last
kiss', from my first love.
The 'beautiful struggle,' girls were my real drug,
fast forward a few years minus a few peers,
This badge has 'all eyez on me' and I can see
clear, with this job

I'm even more of a threat, police work is no different.
It's still about 'money, power, and respect,' I recall this scene
This dude was amped in the hood, him and his team.
He was real live he said, 'we are the streets and we ready to die!'
So, I looked at him dead in his eye, he said, 'even though you twelve
I got respect for you, I ain't gone lie, and I just hate those pigs that mistreat us
Knowing they're soft as pumpkin pie!' They were mad because earlier some cop
Yelled at his mom during a drug bust.
 I talked him down and told him to be easy,
His reply was 'nigga I'm ghetto fabolous,' we dispersed at a fast rate.
You know how cops drive, especially me listening to the purple tape,
I questioned myself "what were you thinking about?
To take a job which involves cases being proved beyond a 'reasonable doubt,'
Sometimes, with words I'm at a loss, as I grip 'God's Son' cross
To protect me in these streets.
It seems everyone hates the cops,

But 'I am' me, I pray my 'life is good' 'til the casket drops.'

WASHED HANDS

I was originally considered one of your own,
Until I made a mistake and now I'm on my own.
No support from my police family and some of
my blood,
Y'all disposed of me with no remorse;
I'm thinking there never was any love.
The news paints a horrific picture of me with
their skewed stories,
I guess I ain't shit that quick after all the good
I've done.
When y'all make the same mistakes as me, but
haven't been caught,
I must be the confused one.
You've finished scrubbing your hands with that
soap?
I'm done!

HIS WORDS

It takes 10 years to be vested in the city,
But it only takes 1 bullet or 1 knife to damage 1
vein
Causing you to lose your 1 life.

-Officer Rich

DEADLY SCENE

Everyone wishes they could take back or change
Things at some in time during their life,
This couldn't be truer than now
Seeing this lifeless body lying on the ground,
The hood all gathered around.
My building, my homies, women and children;
Usually people ain't out here like this unless it's
A party or something,
But it's jumping.
I even saw Ms. June out here
And it seem like she ain't been out here in years,
But it's clear;
This is a fucked up scenario,
With caution tape tied around cars and trees,
And the sight of my mother crying hysterically
Falling to her knees.
With revengeful energy in the air
Given off by the G's,
I'm seeing white faces which are foreign to these
parts.
Cameras rolling, lights flashing and news
anchors broadcasting;
Social media going crazy,
Informing everybody in some form or fashion.
I wanna cry, but I can't, it's like I'm numb

And something told me when I left the crib;
I should grab my gun,
But I was just running outside real quick.
A few minutes at most, that's it.
I never made it back inside,
And it's fucked up looking at the scene,
Where I just died.

#BLACKLIVESMATTER

I saw on the news a black cop shot a black teen;
Who was pointing a gun at the police,
Prior to the shooting,
He posted on social media that
#BLACKLIVESMATTER,
And alluded that no riots or marches
Take place in all black neighborhoods;
When blacks are shooting up each other.
He may have violated his department's social
media policy,
By discussing personal feelings,
But did he violate the truth?

THAT SITUATION

It's all about articulation,
So why put yourself in that situation
No it's not cool for a cop to violate your rights,
Like you a fool
But aggressing on an officer is a fight
You'll most likely lose
I'm not saying be a tool and not exercise your
rights
Instead,
Exercise it in a way that won't risk
Leaving you dead
Why keep your hands in your pockets
When told to reveal them
You may have nothing on you,
But who knows your intentions;
Except for you.
So please no sudden movements or sudden
flinching
Because the objective reasonable belief,
That there's a threat
Can leave you shot in an instance.
How can one determine a cop's reasonable
objectiveness?
A dead person can't talk,
If wrongly arrested for a misdemeanor

At least you can fight that in court.
You're right,
You shouldn't have to go through all that,
And this shouldn't even be an issue.
As with everything else, that's not fair.
All I'm asking, is do what's needed to survive
your encounter with the cop,
You will live to fight another day,
And light a fire to dismantle this sickening plot.

PROTECTION

It's a simple equation that's not simply resolved,
I feel in some cases where black citizens and
white cops are involved,
And unfortunate events occur,
A misunderstanding is the cause.
The cultural backgrounds aren't the same,
And that stems to both party's interaction
Being out of their lane.
It's a shame, for instance, in a majority black
neighborhood; that's low income.
The residents interact with mostly other blacks
and such.
So some may call their general perception of
whites to be out of touch,
Then white cops who never experienced this
environment are thrown into areas,
And aren't accustomed to that dynamic leading
to more barriers.
There's a lot of tension because some view the
officers as 'crooked white cops',
And some officers view the male residents as
'thugs on the block'.
So effective communication suffers
From the lack of respect for authority
To the misinterpretation at times of loud talking,

And body language as active aggression,
To the point where some people feel it's from the officers;
In which they need the protection.

NOT ALL

Finishing the academy and being a new sworn
officer, I didn't know what I was doing.
We go through the academy to get a foundation;
Of law enforcement,
But everyone knows the real training is on the
streets.
Of course, there are more white officers than
black officers.
So during my training phase,
I was trained by white officers.
There's a lot that goes on with enforcing the law;
Laws, ordinances, department directives, etc...
change every day.
So basically, you can easily get in trouble,
Even if you had good intentions,
Because you may simply not know that you're in
violation of something.
Each call is different, regardless if it's classified
as DV call, a noise complaint, a disturbance, a
fight crowd, a robbery, an assault and so forth.
There's a potential for something to occur that
you aren't expecting,
And I can say during my tenure as a cop,
I never got into trouble because those veteran
cops looked out for me.

I went home after every shift and they taught me
what I can or shouldn't do.
So, I won't end up getting jammed up.
Sure, I witnessed some biases and foul stuff in
regards of race,
But the cops I was around looked out for me
And treated people fairly.
I guess the point I'm trying to make,
Is every white cop shouldn't be labeled,
Because of the actions of some other dumb ass
cop.

Amos Mac, Jr.

NO ASSISTANCE

If everyone followed the no snitching rule,
The jails would be empty.
Simply, asking a question without guessing.
I know when cops come around, usually no one
wants to help,
But if a relative is murdered with no leads,
Would you be upset that no one helps?
And regardless of your loss,
Not helping the cops, is how they felt?
Plus, I thought snitching was engaging in an act,
But when you get caught you tell the authorities
the facts.
And the street secrets;
Not giving a tip on a man whose hands land on
his significant other,
Which happens quite frequent,
Maybe it's that you don't snitch, tell or help at
all,
Because if it doesn't affect you and yours,
You feel you shouldn't get involved.

SOCIAL MEDIA

As I view social media,
I can see what's of importance,
But where the hell did we go wrong?
Where the youth's only concerns,
Are fights and the release of the new Jordans.

VIEWS

I hate the fact that hate exists,
From the deepest pits of my being,
And it's alive and well from what I'm seeing;
From human beings.
I hate that today's kids lack respect,
With parents being their friend instead of
putting them in check.
I hate the youth feels being tough is enough,
And you're only relevant;
If you're from a place that's rough.
I hate that pride costs so many lives,
At a price not valued by life.
All of this hate garners more attention than the
positivity;
That we somehow forget to mention.
Is that our intention to stir up conflict?
For drama awards more views,
And we're all being used.
Since the influx of images being spewed,
Subconsciously influences our views,
Sometimes I hate the news.

HAVE THINGS CHANGED

I was having a discussion,
With another brotha on the force about the force.
I'll never forget the look of disgust on his face.
He said, "The police originated as groups of
white motherfuckas chasing and rounding up
slaves.
Look that shit up!
Look at it today, that shit ain't changed!
How is that not the same thing that's going on
right now?!"
I just shook my head and say to myself,
"DAMN!"

PRAYER

Father, I pray that you protect me and my
colleagues as we're working tonight.
I ask that we remain alert, as it's easy to get
caught up in a routine frame of mind,
By going to the same type of calls every day.
I pray for safety and security.
I know this is a type of job that welcomes
conflict,
So, if I happen to be in the midst of altercation,
I pray that I perform to the best of my ability.
I pray that my gun doesn't jam, if I need it
Because lately I've been dreaming that I need it,
but it doesn't work.
I don't know what that means.
I understand I may have to take a life tonight, if
necessary to make it through,
But if my life happens to end, I pray I don't die in
vain.
I pray that you comfort my family and friends
during that time of pain.
I pray that I leave some sort of mark.
I pray that you bless the men and women who
risk their lives,
And sacrifice their families for the well-being of
others.

I pray that I don't turn cold Father, because
lately I can see a change in myself;
I feel I'm starting to reflect the world Father.
I thank you for reading my heart and not my
actions.
I don't want to sound like I'm complaining, but
I'm just talking to You.
I pray that we do an effective job tonight and
understand that this job is about the people.
I pray you give us strength because we're human
and it's not easy dealing with the public,
But it is our job, so I pray we do right by it.
Thank you for all of Your blessings.
In Jesus name I pray,
Amen.

Amos Mac, Jr.

BLACK DEATH

Legend says I was put in the black community,
To run rampant and cause destruction like the
Black Plague.
Turning humans into living zombies,
Destroying families due to me dismantling the
males
Through prison sentences and homicides;
Black Death describes me, pun intended,
But my true color is the opposite.
Some say my insertion into 'the hood',
Simulates the white man's oppression of the
black man in the past;
I was the definition of an epidemic.
However, I'm still alive and well, in all of my
forms
With no means of turning back,
I am Crack.
I'm rocks, I'm coke and any other term you
prefer to use;
I am Black Death.

LOOKS ARE DECEIVING

Police work isn't pretty,
Sometimes there will be blood.
Aggression matched with aggression,
And that's not a delightful sight for the general
public.
There's this view that policing should be all
happy,
But in reality,
There's times where violence is needed,
To stop violence.

NO DIFFERENCE WITH ME

Reality hits when I take the uniform off,
Because when I get pulled over
Or approached by cops, I get the same
mistreatment at times,
As other black males.
When I tell them I'm a cop –
The interrogation really starts as if this can't be
true.
"Oh really?? Which department, let me see your
police ID, which location?"
When I respond with validation, their tone and
responses change.
"Oh if I had known you were a cop..."
Or "I'm sorry brother...."
It shouldn't matter if I'm a cop or not,
For you not to disrespect or mess with me.

SIRENS

It's a rush, swerving like a kid pretending he or
she is flying,
But I'm flying too, only attached to this
pavement,
Because gravity wins the battle of my desire to
take off.
In any other capsule zigzagging in and out of
these lanes,
I would be concerned about the law chasing me;
And there would be some sort of punishment for
not following the rules.
But the lights flashing on top of this mobile
casket is a free pass,
To ignore the posted signage, all I see is brake
lights;
Pulling to the left and right of the avenue.
Paving a clear path in a modern display of
parting the Red Sea,
Along with the alarming signal that help is
coming.
As the thunderous echoes of sirens bounce off of
homes and buildings,
While the Ford is passing, my eyes scan the
laptop;
The road and the traffic simultaneously.

Amos Mac, Jr.

As my ears intake the alerts broadcasted by the
calming voice,
Dispatching through the radio,
It's much to digest while enroute to a priority
call.

ARRESTING JUST BECAUSE

Over the radio, my partner and I heard,
That another unit had arrested someone.
So, we went to their location to see if everything
was 10-4.
Upon arrival we saw an individual,
Who we have had dealings with on a few
accounts.
That subject was standing off to the side.
She is usually drunk when we cross paths,
And it was no different tonight.
We see her then walk to the officers.
We asked if they were good and inquired what
was going on.
One officer informed us the highly intoxicated
lady told them.
That a black male wearing a purple shirt pulled a
knife on her at her near the store.
The officers said they saw a guy wearing a purple
shirt in close proximity to the lady.
They advised they approached the guy asking
him did he have a firearm on him.
They advised he told them he did not know what
they were talking about.

They said they continued questioning and he took off running.
They advised they tackled, cuffed, and placed the man in the back of the cruiser.
My partner asked the officers if they found a knife.
The officers advised he did not have a knife on him
And there wasn't one near the incident location.
My partner then asks why they arrested the guy.
They replied because he ran.
He then said, "How are you going to arrest someone for running?"
He asked what are the charges and one says, "resist."
We shook our heads and drove off.

DUMB CRIMINALS

I've never been a criminal, but one would think,
If you're doing dirt, you'd keep it in the dark.
Nowadays, you have these fools posting
everything on FB and IG,
Why post pics of yourself online showing
evidence?
These geniuses are snitching on themselves,
As Fred Sandford would say, "you big dummy!"

OLD FRIEND

One of my best friends since I was a child;
Who I haven't heard from in a while,
Because his run in's with 'the man',
Left him locked in the can;
Told me something most people wouldn't
understand.
He called me saying he heard I had the badge,
Yea the kid a pig now and we both began to
laugh.
He said regardless, we niggas for life and I'm
proud of you,
If I were in your position, I'd do the same thing
too.
I was surprised at the words he was saying,
I said you know cats kinda acting different,
Now that I'm in this lane.
Fam, you know niggas is lame and everybody
ain't the same,
Just continue to be that stand up dude,
You might be able to change stuff,
So continue to do your thing.
Something I'd never forget,
Some real words from someone who saw me for
me and not the blue line.
For him to know that affected me,

To a point I wrote about him in a book,
Would probably blow his mind.

TORN

I'm torn, often wondering if a revolution or some
sort of civil war will take place;
In the states, in the wake of black dudes dying
from the guns of cops.
Whether or not it may have been justified,
Or the fact that each of you would have done the
same if you wore those shoes.
With the influence of the news instigating
conflict.
I've never had a fro with a pick in it,
But my black pride, wonders if a gun will be
pointed at me.
Saying I should pick sides, it's us or your job,
You can't play both sides of the fence;
But sometimes that makes sense.
When I see brothas dead which could have been
prevented possibly,
Regardless of which side bears the brunt of
responsibility.
And it's like I just sit back and watch since I'm a
cop,
And I'm black which is fact,
Yet in these days that's oil and water,
It doesn't mix, so at times I'm yelling fuck cops,

While I'm a cop because of the stuff I've
experienced
And other times,
I scream fuck us because we plague one another,
destroying our own.
Then I see online black cops getting murdered by
black dudes,
But of course it doesn't make national news.
And I'm more confused,
Because in both scenarios whether being killed
by a cop;
Who's not black or,
Being a black cop shot dead by another black
person
Could be me.

NO PIGS ALLOWED

As I read comments posted on controversial
video links involving cops,
I see posts like 'death to all pigs' or 'the only
good cop is a dead cop' or 'we don't need cops'.
Well, I have a few questions for you;
If you're in a car wreck and your insurance
company needs a police report?
Would you say to them, "nah fuck the police, I
don't need a report;
I'll just use the money out of my pocket to get the
car fixed, don't worry 'bout it"?
That's just a minor scenario.
How about if a gunman goes on a shooting spree
in a public place,
Can the public call on you like you're a
superhero,
And you come running to risk your life in an
effort to stop the gunman?
Or, would you sit back and follow the news
coverage in your safe haven;
Simply commenting on what someone should be
doing;
Or, what should or should not be taking place.
Like you're doing right now?
It's just a question.

WHITE SUIT

An officer tells me he puts on his uniform each
day,
For work like a paycheck slave.
And unless it's safety on the job he's disengaged,
Shucking and jiving every day to get paid.
Yet, his beliefs don't mimic the department's
outlook.
Frustration pumps through his veins with each
beat of his heart,
Wishing he knew what he was getting himself
into from the start.
Each time he arrives home from his shift,
He's hesitant to look in the mirror;
And each day it becomes more clearer,
How his strings are being pulled.
He tells me he dreams of another way of life,
And in pursuit because he's exhausted of putting
on and taking off,
The "white suit"

Mac, Jr.

LETTER TO MA

Dear Ma,
He Mama, how are you doing?
I know I'm your baby,
The youngest of your children
And we have a special bond.
I've always wanted to make you proud of me.
I miss the innocence of being a child
And reminisce of childhood memories
With your influence embedded in it.
I wonder what goes through your mind
When I come home and lay my head on your lap
As a grown man.
Ma, I think about you all the time
And I know I should call much more often than I
do.
I will do a better job of that.
I know you worry about me
At time especially with my profession.
I see the look in your eyes
When I speak and it shows concern
As if your baby is changing,
Not necessarily for the better.
Ma, I'm fine

And I'm going to be everything you prayed I
would be.
Life is a difficult Ma,
Something you are well aware of obviously.
I'm trying to claw myself through these webs in
life and I struggle.
Why am I even here and not my twin?
Why did I survive?
What am I supposed to offer the world?
I feel like I have great potential,
But I'm not living up to it.
You told me you didn't think law enforcement
was for me,
So I can understand your fears.
You wisdom is far beyond my comprehension
and I,
At times, still don't listen like when I was a child.
It seems like I would have learned by now, right?
I remember you telling me
That your baby doesn't sound the same.
I'm good now Ma, please don't worry about me.
Thank you for being my mother.
I can never express my gratitude enough.
If only I could take all of your pain away.
I'm coming home soon.
See ya Ma, love you!!!!

Amos Mac, Jr.

NOT FREE

I'm not free in America, the land of the free,
I'm not free from the burdens that haunt me;
Each day it reminds me I can chase my dreams.
Yet, I'll never escape the curses of this soil,
Because I'm blessed with this skin.
I can't escape being picked on as a child,
Because my skin is dark.
Beautiful, though I may add, only jokes I know,
But the root of it is much darker because jokes
carry some truth.
And the truth being, my people have been
brainwashed over the years,
To actually feel being lighter is more beneficial in
society.
This leads to a young sista in high school saying;
"She can't date a brotha",
Because their skin doesn't match.
What type of thought process is that?
I can't escape a non-supportive community that
will make other races rich,
And complain that we don't have anything.
I'm not free from being just another
'nigga/nigger',
I'm a 'sellout ass nigga' and a 'nigger in uniform'.

Nah fuck that, I'm a man that was born not to be the norm,
Yet, I'm not free,
I'M NOT FREE....
From the incarceration rates, the racism hidden in plain sight.
The products of white privilege, the homicide rates,
The homicide statistics in the black community, the injustices displayed daily.
The idea we are the blame for our circumstances;
The attitude of not aspiring to do better,
Because of the cards that were dealt.
Not realizing it was a misdeal and being satisfied with settling.
The dream is lost because one can't envision it.
Due to the lack of relatable representation through sight,
I am free to write this,
But my lack of freedom,
Is the reason I wrote it.

REBELLION

Blood puddles everywhere with bodies, Sprawled
lifeless where children play.
The agonizing sounds of family members,
Weeping over their fallen relatives,
Serve as a continuous soundtrack of these
dreadful times.
Endless fighting in the streets with no peace
treaty in sight,
And each individual being forced to fight
whether they desire to or not.
This reality is far more horrific than The Walking
Dead,
This war began because the people were tired of
viewing black people killed;
Beaten, and mistreated at the hands of white
officers with no retribution.
They began to rebel, as if following the influence
of the German Coast Uprising.

I wrote the above passage, because I feel that one day the people will take matters into their own hands. With everything seen today, there is no faith in the judicial system, because there is a feeling that justice does not apply when it comes to African-Americans in this country. It seems we may be on the verge of civil unrest where destruction of property; due to looting and burning may continue, but carnage may take place. Hopefully it doesn't come to this, but I have a feeling if something doesn't change it could be looming.

ATTENTION ATTRACTED

Around 1 am there was a robbery call,
Which occurs often in that area,
Being broadcasted over the radio,
Relaying the suspect's description.
Units were being assigned to the call.
Another unit and I circulated the incident parameter,
And approached a subject on foot.
We made sure he didn't have any weapons
By frisking him.
Information was gathered, by asking him a few questions;
To see if there were any consistencies with him and the comments in the call.
His name was also run in the system to see if he had warrants.
He was cooperative and was not the suspect in question.
As we were about to leave, the subject asks,
"Why do cops always approach me like I fit the description or something?"
I said, "What do you think the description is?"
He replied, "A black male, wearing a white tee, jeans."

I responded with, "Well that kinda answered your question because you just described yourself."

He then said, "Well just because I wear this doesn't mean I'm a criminal or suspect! That's fucked up."

I said, "I couldn't agree with you more, but just realize what comes with that."

He looked puzzled and replied, "What you mean?"

I said, "Outside of this uniform other cops don't know,

That I'm an officer especially when I'm wearing fitteds, studs and jewelry.

I've been approached by cops before because I fit a description.

What I'm basically saying is even though it's not fair or right,

Understand that you attract certain attention with your appearance,

Especially, out here at 1 in the morning."

Amos Mac, Jr.

POPS

What's going on dad?
I'm seeing things as an adult and it's real sad.
You told me when I was a child
I should be thankful to have a father in my life;
and I am.
I know your dad wasn't in your life
And it takes a real dude not to follow that same
path.
You taught me how to be a man.
Told me I better not quit and showed me the
value of hard work.
These are traits I see lacking in the young
generation of dudes.
I still tell people about the stories I heard about
you from back in the day.
Cats laugh about it because apparently your
name carried weight
And nobody would know that by meeting you
now.
That shows how you've evolved over the years.
I know we had a rough patch at one point when I
was in high school,
But that was petty.
Everybody say you spit me out

And when I was young I didn't like that, but now I'm proud.

Thank you for exposing me to a two-parent home.

Thank you for whooping my ass and not sparing the rod

Because from what I see on a daily basis, a lot of these folks needed that.

I don't know where I'd be if you weren't in my life.

Maybe I would be in the system like some of the other dudes from the neighborhood.

Who knows?

But old ma, chill out though because you're in your 60s now

And working 12 plus hours a shift at a factory.

I know that's crucial. I wish I could be more of a help

And take you out of that situation.

I'm sorry that I can't.

Love you pops.

Amos Mac, Jr.

PREDESTINATION

In my line of work,
I've dealt with many juveniles.
Whose family background consist of
Drug addiction, hustling, jail, gangs, etc.
Interacting with them causes me to question
What I once believed.
I used to feel there wasn't such a thing as
predestination,
But at times now I question it.
Children are sponges who absorb their
environment.
So, what are the odds that the children won't
Follow in the same footsteps?
I also have another question,
Is this really a question of predestination or
Is it actually part of plan which was instituted
generations ago?

TRAPPED

I dislike being a cop now.
I really don't believe in this.
Other than a salary what will I really achieve
with this?
I may bleed with this.
May be able to support my seed with this,
But will I be able to succeed with this?
Like being at peace with this.
Not stressed a lot and get some pleasant sleep
with this.
Who even speaks like this?
I'm talking to myself, but I sound like a creep
with this.
Coworkers asking, "What else competes with
this?
How can anyone consider leaving this?"
Am I ungrateful, because many others live for
this?
I see, I'm just not built for this.
My faith here doesn't exist.
So, I'm not risking being killed for this.
I see innocent blood being spilled with this.
Clearly it's not my calling,
So my progression begins to yield with this.

I put some years in this.
My love ones prayed daily, because of their fear
with this.
I began to change over the years with this.
When I say goodbye.
You truly won't be missing this.

HOW FAST IS 911

The notion that police arrive faster in white
neighborhoods than other neighborhoods,
It's somewhat true, well at least from my
experience.
Why is that?
Because there is more patrol units in these areas,
Than areas considered low income areas.
So, when 911 calls are placed here;
Cops arrive fast because there's not much going
on in these areas.
As far as street crime,
On the flip side, there are less cops working the
high crime areas.
So, the cops are stretched thin running from call
to call,
Thus causing them to arrive late.
The real question is, why is this allowed to
happen?
It seems that one's social class determines,
The importance of one's safety,

Amos Mac, Jr.

BIGGEST WEAPON

During my days in the police academy,
I don't recall much of the chatter spewed at me,
But I do recall what this one black officer said
and the concept wasn't new to me.
Brutally, honest he said,
"A cop's biggest weapon isn't that night stick and
It ain't the taser, or the pepper spray,
It's not the flashlight or the pistol fed with lead,
It's not even a knife."
He advised,
It's your fucking mouth that may save your life.
That hole can talk you in or out of a fight.
It can build rapport with citizens, who in turn
will value your life.
You can go from being viewed as the typical cop;
To them saying, "You know what? That officer
right there is alright!"
Death can come in an instance, with ambush
tactics,
But it's been times where citizens informed
officers of the hit.
This prevented that officer's murder from
happening.

With that being said, I'll never forget that message;
I wonder how many of my peers absorbed that lesson.

Amos Mac, Jr.

WORTH IT

I wonder what my life is worth,
To my family, you can't place value on my worth.
For my mom, though her life was worth my
birth,
But as a cop, to the public now my life is a curse.
A dead cop is celebrated by some;
Like winning the lotto,
And some remember the dead by pouring drink
out the bottle.
Some look at taking a life simply as earning a
stripe
While some view death just as part of this game
called life
So does it make it easy to kill a man you caught
in bed with your wife?
Or murk someone who disrespected you in front
of your boys last night?
There are many reasons some may see fit for the
killing season
I guess the value of life depends on the price
Willing to be paid whether here on Earth or the
afterlife
By each person
As a man who advocates life preserving
If one has to die in order to protect a person

How do you determine whose life is worth it?

Amos Mac, Jr.

QUESTIONS FOR YOU OFFICER

Officer, I know you have a very difficult and
thankless job in general,
But I want to ask you some questions on your
current situation.
With everything being displayed in the news and
on social media,
Depicting all officers as trained killers.
I just wanted to pick your brain;
As to how do you go about working these
protests as a black cop?
How do you feel about the protesters,
Who question your blackness?
Do you feel you should join the protest,
Instead of working there as a cop?
Does working the protest make you question,
Why continue being an officer?
When the protesters are yelling at you and don't
appreciate what you are trying to bring to the
community,
How does that make you feel?
Do the protests make you look at the community
differently?
If it weren't for your family,
Would you quit or look to transfer?
If the last question wasn't the case,

Does your family actually push you to resign?
Do you feel your coworkers understand your
position?
If you could be completely honest and not have
to be concerned with any repercussions,
What would you say?

Amos Mac, Jr.

PSALM 46:1

Do I believe in God or guns?
I believe if it came down to it,
God will guide my aim.

IMPACT

You will never know what type of an impact you
will make on people's lives when being an officer.
I was told,
I didn't realize this until I encountered this one
17 year old.
I met him the second week of me patrolling on
the streets.
Riding with my training officer,
I had no clue what to do.
We went on every type of call,
So I can get some experience.
From missing persons and larcenies to any call
involving a dead body,
Whether natural or homicide.
Got the experience of going to court,
And was always made to do all the reports.
Along with all sorts of extras,
I guess that was me paying my dues,
Seeing if I could fill my shoes.
I recall this 17 year old lying,
Accusing someone of shooting into his house
But after some investigation, it was him that shot
the gun;
Officers figured it out.

He discharged it on accident and the projectiles
shattered some glass.
And he tried to conceal the small pistol,
Underneath some trash.
I pulled him outside and spoke to him for about
30 minutes;
Gave him some advice, encouraged him,
Told him he could do better.
Just reality talk about life,
Nothing too clever.
I thought he wasn't really listening,
Only nodding his head.
Fast forward 2 years later,
A guy spoke to me and surprisingly said,
"Hey! We met before do you remember?
It was a couple of years ago sometime in
November.
I'm the guy who shot the gun in the house,
And I listened to everything you were talking
about.
I changed my act up and now I got a job,
Thanks for the talk that day
I've never interacted with a cop that way."
I was shocked that he actually listened.
Those words resonated about me making an
impact,
Needless to say, I was joyed

Knowing that I did give back that day.

Amos Mac, Jr.

GOOD NEWS ISN'T NEWS

Views around 30K and steadily climbing,
On a virtual book composed of pictures.
Videos and an infinite amount of words
broadcasted,
As millions of people take advantage of this
online stage.
This one particular episode illustrates an officer
doing his job;
By assisting a woman in danger
And saves her from injury,
Courtesy of this footage was captured
By an intelligent, mobile communication device,
Other such devices were used to witness the
show.
As well as, serve as a medium to voice their
opinions on what they viewed.
Consistently, viewers commented with a sort of
relieved tone.
That it was about time an officer did their job,
And there are a few good cops left out here.
While cops, such as myself, realize these events
occur every day,
Yet understand good deeds, in general,
Aren't highlighted as much as something
negative

Let alone aspects of police work

Amos Mac, Jr.

BRAINLESS COPS

Dumb is one word that doesn't describe me,
So, when we interact, don't assume this cop
Doesn't have the intellect to be in your presence
And question your actions simply, because you
think I'm not educated.
Due to my current occupation;
I'm not a genius, true indeed,
But I do have papers, suggesting I had some sort
of
Mental aptitude to undergo higher learning,
And depart by strutting across the stage
After my name was called.
Besides insulting me on my brain capacity,
You take aim at my livelihood.
Insinuating my salary is paid by you, because
you pay taxes
But I pay taxes as well, so the question is;
Do I actually pay myself to deal with you and
your foolishness on a daily basis?
Clearly this sort of job isn't going anywhere.
In retrospect, maybe you were right to believe
I suffer from a lack of intelligence.
You're correct, one has to be silly to be
underpaid,

To make sacrifices for strangers and never
shown appreciation.
It's senseless to desire protecting people,
And come to their aid when most won't.
I guess the lives of the public are trivial matters,
Taken on by us brainless cops

CONFUSED ADMIRATION

Admiration can be defined as a feeling of
approval or wonder.
Somewhere along those lines, and I'm trying,
To figure out if admiration and hate go together
hand and hand.
Like disliking an athlete, but you continue to
watch,
He or she in the hopes of their failure.
Meanwhile, you're still supporting them,
Which in turn makes you a fan in a sense.
Admiration can lead one to do things out of
character.
Ironically, no one likes the police.
Yet, you often see individuals who say that,
Pushing old police cruisers down the street,
Or certain guns being sought after,
Because "That's what 'troll' holds".
Even neighborhood security wants to be down,
To the point where they confront teens;
And leave them dead on the ground.

WHY SO IMPORTANT

I look around and wonder why my service is even
needed here today,
Why is it like this with my people?
Why are we the only ones here today?
On the verge of rioting, yelling and being
disruptive; some of us officers were hired today
to 'keep the peace.'
You would think someone was giving away
money, the way people are standing out here.
How can this be a top priority?
Do we flock to this, because it assists our social
status and we want to appear as though we have
money?
Lives at times have been lost in an effort to own
it. Bills haven't been paid, yet we fiend for it like
it's a drug.
I've never understood getting a raffle to spend
my own money.
Why is this so important?
It shouldn't come to cops having to work at
stores, during the releasing of Jordans.

GUNS

There's been a push for strict gun laws,
But I feel this only affects law abiding citizens,
Not the criminals at all.
Guns flood the streets and anybody can get them
for cheap,
Whether it's a kid, an adult, gangs, or any person
in general.
Why make it difficult for 'good guys' to legally
obtain firearms?
When they're the ones needed for the armed
criminals.

I'M OFF

I'm human, so I will make some mistakes.
It's like the concerns of my personal life,
Fused with the stress of work;
Won't give me a break.
You want me to solve your problems,
When I can't even solve my own,
And I'm frustrated with adults acting like
children, knowing they're grown.
I dislike talking on the phone now,
Because I realize it's another pipeline of
problems being relayed.
It's like I can't escape it and I hate it.
Let me chill, give myself a little time to build.
I know mediating is my job,
But when I'm off,
Monitor your mouth and understand;
You're problems aren't what I'm trying to talk
about.

Amos Mac, Jr.

MY JOB II

The idea of wearing the shield is not typically
ideal, for the masses more so blasphemous,
For the actions seen on screen whether
television, cell phone or computer.
Being an officer is a thought that very few can get
used to,
Read the comments on YouTube,
Although not very useful
Similar to tools,
I'm used to getting used too.
My actions though are fruitful.
You question my duties in most cases,
Rudely and when it's beneficial to you,
Is the only time your plans include me.
In turn, leave my job to me and I'll leave yours to
you.
Who cares if you yell, do it 'til you turn blue.
I answer to very few and those few are never you.

WHAT'S THE DIFFERENCE

Working on the wealthy side of the city one
night,
I went to a commercial alarm call.
An alarm was triggered at a CVS.
A few officers made entry into the building to see
if anyone was inside.
There was an elderly lady standing in the
entrance of the store.
She had been shopping.
The employees of the store had locked the store
with the subject still inside.
As we spoke to her she advised,
She wanted to leave a note on her shopping
basket;
Full of items to inform the staff,
She will return in the morning to purchase those
items inside the basket.
After contacting the store manager and clearing
the call,
I couldn't help from laughing and telling people
about it.
As I reflected on it though,
I thought about the dynamics of that situation.
If this occurred on the side of town where I
patrol, what would have happened?

Am I wrong to feel someone would have come
into the store and stolen something?
Why would the scenario be different,
If any, on a low income part of town?
Is it because there's so much lack in those areas?
And the people here want for nothing?
So basically, is the majority of crime spurned by
residents who struggle financially?
And don't have much?
What do you think?

HOLLYWOOD

I'm ready for Hollywood,
And I've been cast to play the leading role in
'Eagle Eye'.
I'm dressed to impress,
With my uniform pressed and all lights are on
me.
Everywhere I turn paparazzi is there,
With their camera phones flashing snapping
pictures and recording.
I never see images of me in magazines,
Where I'm all made up and jazzy.
Instead, it's only raw footage of me in action,
Where I'm portrayed as a villain.
I'm supposed to be the hero in this role,
But directors behind the cameras paint a rob
zombie worthy collage of my takes.
I'm on guard because if I make the slightest
mistake, my face is on display.
There's word that the public wants a POV cam on
my body while I'm acting.
I'm anxious to see the paparazzi's acting,
When my camera is filming them.
I wonder will this cause my current images,

To clean up when my cameras capture you acting.

WORTH

I've often wondered,
What's the value of life here in America?
I once thought that no value can be placed on a
human's life.
After my short stint on this realm,
Experiencing news coverages, judicial hearings,
public opinion, etc,
I've realized a person's worth in America,
Is based a lot upon net worth.
Money and popularity determines one's
importance.

GANG

A group or band is an easy way to describe a
gang. They wear colors,
Roll in packs,
Run their area or turf,
Carry weapons,
Have governing rules,
And have a power structure.
Gangs have their own slang,
Codes and initiations.
Gang affiliation is a lifestyle,
And has its own culture.
I joined the biggest gang in the city
When I took that oath,
And my life ain't been the same since.

WHO I AM

Amos Mac Jr is you and I.

Amos is everyone.

And represents a voice that needs to be heard about life's circumstances.

This voice shines light on the cries that have gone silent.

Everyone relates to this voice.

Amos Mac, Jr.

RANT

Another African-American was unjustly slain by
the hands of a white cop.
Why do we act surprised?
This has been going on for years,
But I guess it hits home now,
Because we can visually see the footage of the
dead bodies lying in the street.

The same day a black person murdered another
black person.
Did this incident get the same news press?
Not likely, because the media decides a white
officer killing a black man;
Is more newsworthy,
Thus promoting a race war.

We complain about police mistreatment,
Yet, we continue to call them.
What happened to policing our own
neighborhoods?
We don't want cops around,
But we invite them in.
I'm a cop and I won't call 911,
Unless it's something completely out of my
hands.

Community policing is dying,
Because officers today are foreign;

Meaning, numerous officers aren't policing in
areas they grew up in.
I'm guilty of this.
So what do I have in common with my patrol
Area residents other than my race?
The community doesn't know, officers anymore.
Hence there's a disconnect,
Growing more rapid with police and community.

Marching isn't solving anything.
The only item all people pay attention to is
money.
We make everyone rich but ourselves,
So, take the money out of their pockets
And make our demands.

Supporting each other is not an option either,
I guess.
Other races will go into business,
Together and have a few shops within a strip
mall,
Sharing the profit, but what do we do?
Open up a corner store, that's booming within
the neighborhood,
But won't expand because we're not supporting.

I'm trying to think of another race,
Who has an appointed spokesperson for the
masses?
We do though.
How is it that Sharpton is always speaking for all
of us?

We're so far in the hole.
Us, men are attacked on the physical front.
Just look at the jail tragedy,
Police brutality,
And warring against each other.
So, our power is broken down.
A lot of us now, don't want to be with our own
women.
What's wrong with us?
The women are attacked mentally.
They're image is lost
And they don't respect their natural beauty,
Because that fake imagery is more appealing in
society's eyes.
Many sisters don't want us either.
It's like we're awaiting liberation or something.
How do we expect or desire other races to fix
ours?

SIGN UP!

Calling all African Americans!
Your help is needed!
Before the force can be complete,
We need you to sign up to patrol the streets.

More 'minorities' need to be hired,
So law enforcement appears to promote equality.
Besides, many blacks suggest;
Having black officers patrolling black
neighborhoods would be best.

What a great opportunity for public servants.
I mean, public service to assist the community by
giving back.
Being ostracized by your own community will
happen,
But that's okay, you'd be a cop,
So you can live with that.

You'd be arresting many more blacks than
whites,
That's part of your job requirements, so you
should sleep peaceful at night.
Your inner 'uncle ruckus' will shine bright,
As you place those metal bracelets on niggas and
usher them to the can.
Where prison guards and correctional officers
Have been known to be members of the klan,

But that's fine because we offer a great benefits
package.
You have the opportunity to risk your life from
day one,
But as you fight to survive;
Understand you won't be eligible for full benefits
until after year five.
Well, probably more, but who's keeping score.

Moving right along.
After retirement, you won't have paid life
insurance,
But you can work off duty to make more money.
Since technically, your life isn't worth shit as the
salary suggests,
This provides a chance to make ends meet;
By working tons of hours and often missing
putting your kids to sleep.

Join us! What is better than this?
You're already public enemy number one by
being black;
Now you'll have a badge and be a target on two
fronts,
How exciting is that?

Whites won't respect your authority,
You'd be thrown to the wolves, working marches
and protests.
Oftentimes, backing something you don't agree
with, for what?
Ah yes, the check!

We understand the visions you've seen on TV,
In regards to officers and your race,
But let's be honest, they deserved it.
The cops were doing their job.
So, be a good little black person
And stay in your place.

Did I mention, you'd be part of a brotherhood?
Where the sergeant tells you to get those
'motherfuckers' out of the hospital,
And those 'motherfuckers' are family of the
homicide victim.
And the reason they're at the hospital is because
you tricked them.

You told them the victim was transported by the
ambulance.
But, in fact,
He was already dead, the ambulance only drove
around the corner.
Understand we follow strict protocol and have
our reasons for doing that.

Of course the victim and his family was black,
But that's alright, we have to hurt feelings at
times.
And if I were to mention we'd do the same to a
wealthy family in the hospital,
I'd most likely be lying.

You're going to get blamed anytime a cop does
something,

Even if you aren't involved;
You're going to be the scapegoat regardless.
You can do great things,
But the public's perception of you will continue
to be garbage.

We want you to be a robot and do as we say;
Leave you emotionless,
Because feelings only get in the way.
Turn a blind eye at times when your brother or
sister mistreats a citizen,
Especially, one of your own kind.

But, keep in mind you better do as told,
Because misery of the job will unfold.
From you coworkers going against you,
To being held hostage on third shift.
Don't even think about parting your lips to voice
your opinion,
You'll only be the department's minion;
Never involved in the real decisions.

So hurry now and sign up!
We're looking for fools like you,
To represent this prestigious career,
And become a nigger in blue.

SORRY

A feeling of helplessness curses my body,
And my mind is confined by internal blame;
I'm supposed to be a cop.
People dial my 3 digit number when they need
assistance.

I'm apologizing to you, but my words will never
reach your ears.
I'm so sorry I wasn't able to do more
Your eyes told me everything I needed to know,
But I'm restricted by the laws of this land

I hate domestic violence calls,
Because these deep rooted issues never are
solved in one day.
Still though, I shed a tear because I should have
saved you.
You wanted out, but the escape route was too
time consuming.

I still remember our conversation the other day,
I can't believe your child is motherless now.
I'm going crazy and can't stop thinking and
seeing your troubled face.

I wish I could've...I just, should've...
I'm so sorry.
I'm sorry, I'm fucking sorry!!!

FAREWELL

I just wanted to share my voice,
Even though you may never understand my
position.
From my homeboy catching felonies, to me
paying tuition;
Committing the cardinal sin in an effort to better
my nutrition.
I'm pained by my people's struggle,
Entertainment, sports and drugs appear to be
the only hustle
For a lot in their minds.
With gun and liquor stores more accessible than
jobs,
Of course, people turn to crime.
I witness it from both sides of the line.
On one side, I'm fighting the struggle
And the other,
I'm supposedly fighting this ingrained crime.
At the same time,
I'm out!

ARTICULATION

A Short Story

On Tuesday, March 10, 2015 I, Officer Mac, was dispatched to a domestic disturbance call located at 10613 Energy Canon Front Ave. I was operating patrol unit *000*. Prior to arriving on scene I was advised by dispatch that officers have been to this address on many occasions. The complainant advised dispatch the male party involved is a large black male who has a lengthy record involving resist, robbery, carrying a concealed weapon, and breaking and entering.

The remarks in the call advised the male has a warrant and had been confirmed. The remarks also advised the male is very aggressive and had been drinking. The complainant advised the male does not have any weapons that she is aware of but does not know if any is in the house. She advised he has been known to carry a gun. The remarks advised the male was very irate and the call with the complainant was disconnected abruptly and there was no answer on call back.

Upon arrival on scene officers heard a loud disturbance coming from the address listed above. Officers knocked on the door and a female opened the door and ran out of the apartment yelling 'That's him, he hit me!". She advised no other residents were inside the place. We saw a large black male wearing a big coat and baggy pants. The subject was identified as Ryanneek ******. His street name is "Wheels." We asked the male subject were there any weapons inside of the residence. The subject did not respond to our question. We said again are there any weapons in the house because this is for your safety and ours. The subject was very irate and said fuck us. The subject advised he didn't care what we said.

The subject was approximately 6 feet tall and 285 pounds in weight. He was not complying with any commands. The subject was sweating and pacing back and forth. We did not know if he was only under the influence of alcohol or not. With the subject's history with law enforcement we understood the subject may be non-compliant. We did not know if there were any weapons concealed on his person. We knew he had a warrant on file and that we had to take him into custody. Officers advised him he had a warrant and tried to calm him down by talking to him.

We advised we had to detain him. Officer

Smith continued to talk to him in a calm manner to put the subject at ease and to defer any altercation.

Officer Smith is approximately 5'9" in height and approximately 160 pounds. I am 5'8" in height and approximately 175 in weight. We knew it would be difficult to subdue the subject. The subject continued yelling that he's not going to jail and we're not taking him in. Officer Smith communicated to me that a taser would mostly likely be ineffective due to the subject wearing the large coat. For our safety we approached the subject because we did not want to give him more time to think of ways to possibly injure us since he was determined not to go to jail. We knew backup was on the way we felt we needed to address the subject then because continuing to stall may have been costly to our safety.

I went to grab the subject's left arm and Officer Smith went to grab his right arm. We advised him he was under arrest and to put his hands behind his back. As Officer Smith attempted to grab his right arm he shoved Officer Smith in his chest with both of his hands. I grabbed his left forearm with my right hand and the subject attempted to strike me in the face with a clenched fist. Officer Smith then tried to take the subject to the ground by tackling him in the legs. The subject crouched down to make his base stronger, thus preventing Officer Smith from taking him to the ground. The subject grabbed Officer Smith in a manner to detach Officer Smith from his legs and wrestle him to the ground. I then struck the subject in the left side of his face with my clenched hands approximately 2 times.

The subject was very strong. We commanded the subject numerous times to stop resisting. I continued striking the subject in his body with clenched fist so he would let hold of Officer Smith. The subject began to turn his body sideways where his left side of the body was exposed and his right side was being protected. He moved in a manner as if he was protecting something. We felt that he was concealing and reaching for a weapon. Officer Smith was no longer in the subject's grasp. Officer Smith yelled the subject was reaching into the right side of his pants. Officer Smith drew his firearm and commanded the subject to show his hands. The subject did not adhere to Officer Smith's command. The subject continued to yell at his us fuck us. His eyes were glossy as if giving a blank stare the entire time. He commanded for the subject to show his hands for the safety of everyone or he will shoot. The subject didn't comply. Officer Smith fired two rounds into the subject's stomach and chest area. The subject hit the floor and was cuffed. I advised over the radio that shots were fired and were officer involved. I advised dispatch to start medic and the subject had been shot twice. I advised dispatch that no officer had been shot. No weapon was found in the pants of the subject.

This scenario isn't true, but it shows how things can transpire on calls. Some readers may not agree with Officer Smith and Officer Mac's actions, but this shows how an officer may articulate their actions. This is just an example showing details of articulating an action which can lead to an officer not being arrested for shooting an unarmed subject. I know some feel this scenario is debatable and others may see it as clear cut. It's something to think about.